*Life itself remains a
very effective therapy.*

— *Karen Horney*

THE PROMISE OF LIFE

ROGER PRESCOTT

**SERMONS FOR THE
FIRST HALF OF PENTECOST**

C.S.S. Publishing Company
Lima, Ohio

THE PROMISE OF LIFE

Copyright © 1984 by
The C.S.S. Publishing Company, Inc.
Lima, Ohio

All rights reserved. No portion of this book may be reproduced or utilized in any form or by any means, electronic or mechanical including photocopying, without permission in writing from the publisher. Inquiries should be addressed to: The C.S.S. Publishing Company, Inc., 628 South Main Street, Lima, Ohio 45804.

4859/ISBN 0-89536-683-5   PRINTED IN U.S.A.

To my grandchildren:
Angela, Jennette, David, Jr., Tanya and Megan
Who help us, by their examples,
to move though life with a hop,
skip and jump — and some heavenly
class.

Table of Contents

Preface   9

The Day of Pentecost   *Acts 2:1-21*   *All Together*   11

The Holy Trinity   *Isaiah 6:1-8*   *Standing in Awe*   16

Proper 4/Ordinary Time 9 (May 29 — June 4)   *1 Samuel 16:1-13*   *God's Choice*   20

Proper 5/Ordinary Time 10 (June 5-11)   *1 Samuel 16:14-23*   *How To Be Used By God*   25

Proper 6/Ordinary Time 11 (June 12-18)   *2 Samuel 1:1, 17-27*   *A Royal Lament*   30

Proper 7/Ordinary Time 12 (June 19-25)   *2 Samuel 5:1-12*   *The Establishment of an Empire*   35

Proper 8/Ordinary Time 13 (June 26 — July 2)   *2 Samuel 6:1-15*   *Celebration as Worship*   40

Proper 9/Ordinary Time 14 (July 3-9)   *2 Samuel 7:1-17*   *God Dwells With People*   44

Proper 10/Ordinary Time 15 (July 10-16)   *2 Samuel 7:18-29*   *A Prayer of Wonder*   48

Proper 11/Ordinary Time 16 (July 17-23)   *2 Samuel 11:1-15*   *Feet of Clay*   52

Proper 12/Ordinary Time 17 (July 24-30)   *2 Samuel 12:1-14*   *The Promise of Life*   57

Proper 13/Ordinary Time 18 (July 31 — August 6)   *2 Samuel 12:15b-24*   *Back in the Swing*   61

Proper 14/Ordinary Time 19   *Human Nature Revisited*   66
(August 7-13)   *2 Samuel 18:1, 5, 9-15*

Proper 15/Ordinary Time 20   *A Grief Observed*   72
(August 14-20)   *2 Samuel 18:24-33*

Proper 16/Ordinary Time 21   *An Unusual Legacy*   77
(August 21-27)   *2 Samuel 23:1-7*

Acknowledgments   82

Preface

The world is always going through what historian Arnold Toynbee has described as "the painfulness of being human." I hope this little volume can help take some of the sharp edges from that pain. Scripture has a way of doing that. I find that I have been smoothed and nourished as I have developed these sermons.

You will not find critical treatment of the biblical narratives here, though I spent considerable time studying what the scholars have said. Rather, I have tried to find their message for their day, our day, and all the days to come. "Snatching the eternal out of the desperately fleeting," says Tennesee Williams, "is the great magic trick of human existence." The careful study of the Scriptures will help us do that.

In over twenty years as a parish and itinerant preacher, I have never doubted the importance of preaching. I enjoy preaching and I enjoy preparing to preach. And I like to do sometimes as Frederick Buechner says: "make words (and ideas) sing out and dance a little."

The messages that comprise this volume have been developed just as I have developed sermons for more than two decades of living — under the shadow of next Sunday's sermon. A clear outline, two or three clear points, a few illustrations and stories from literature and life, and perhaps some poetry. I hope some of the ideas highlighted here, and filtered through my mind, will stir new thoughts in you — and perhaps even bring a measure of peace as encounter with Scripture unfolds.

I have tried to hear and always keep in mind some of the recurrent themes of Scripture:

1. God accomplishes his plans in spite of us, not because of us.

2. God's revelation takes place within human history — in the lives of real people and concrete relationships and in definite historic periods.

3. God's grace continually adapts to our human frailty.

4. The goodness of God, the joy of life, the bitterness of grief and the power and glory of love are all things expressed through the people of Scripture — and the people of our present world.

After Nathan, the Prophet, had confronted David for his adultery and murder, David had his ears and eyes opened and he repented. David said to

Nathan, "I have sinned against the Lord." And then Nathan said to David, "The Lord also has put away your sin; you shall not die." (2 Samuel 12:13) That chunk of grace is "The Promise of Life" for David. It is our promise too.

May this little volume bring out from "under the edges of the ordinary," a little better glimpse of our reason for existence, through the people of Israel; through the life of Jesus Christ; and through our common humanity.

Roger Prescott

Easter, 1984

The Day of Pentecost
Acts 2:1-21

All Together

Introduction

This is a sermon about *community*. "When the day of Pentecost had come, *they were all together* in one place." (Acts 2:1)

There's a whole lot to this narrative of the Day of Pentecost, but none of it, it seems, would have happened without the disciples being all together — in community. There are at least three things about "community" (read that "church") which it is helpful to remember:

1. Community can be difficult

The German philosopher Schopenhauer once said that people are rather like a pack of porcupines on a freezing winter night. The sub-zero temperature forces them together for warmth. But as soon as they press very close, they jab and hurt one another. So they separate, only to attempt, in vain, over and over again, to huddle together. Togetherness *can* be painful. But without it we will freeze. Certainly the early church had as many difficult people as do our congregations today. In my first congregation, in the north woods of Minnesota, there was an old gentleman who, I thought, made my ministry much harder. He was like the old-timer who, approaching his his ninetieth birthday, was being interviewed. "I suppose there have been a lot of changes in your lifetime," remarked the reporter. The old-timer replied, "There shore have, and I've been again' every blasted one of 'em!" We smile at that, but any pastor will tell you stories about the irascibility of at least one of her or his members. Community can be difficult.

2. Community can be wonderful

Community has to be a place for give and take. For where two or three gather together — someone is sure to spill the milk. Yet the Incarnation calls for the earthy togetherness real living demands. The church at its earliest was not perfect. Neither is it today (or will it be tomorrow). But there is a winsomeness about God's people gathering together. Sometimes parish newsletters put you right to sleep. But once in a while something sparkles in them. Here's an example that ties in with our thinking about community:

Perfect Church

*I think that I shall never see
A church that's all it ought to be;
A church whose members never stray
Beyond the straight and narrow way!
A church that has no empty pews,
Whose pastor never has the blues,
A church whose deacons always deak
And none is proud, and all are meek;
Where gossips never peddle lies,
Or make complaints or criticize;
Where all are always sweet and kind
And to all others' faults are blind.
Such perfect churches there may be,
But none of them are known to me.
But still we'll work and pray and plan
To make our own the best we can.*

Author unknown — *From the South Pacific ALC District Newsletter, June 1975*

Whenever we get irritated by too much togetherness in our community (town, church, family), and familiarity digs its claws into us, we need to re-read and recall this Pentecost narrative.

Without the togetherness, it appears, the Spirit would not have come with comfort, wildness and strength. The next time you see and hear a gathering singing "Happy Birthday" to one of its members, recall that community can be wonderful — and visualize the Spirit being present. Community can be wonderful! These first two concepts (the difficulty and wonder of community) are captured in just a few words by Richard John Neuhaus:

> *The best understanding, of course, is that which holds in one thought the majesty of the Church catholic and the troublesome little band of people at Third Methodist. The communal intuition on which they act may not be legitimated by the Christian teaching they hear. As mentioned before, in that teaching the Church may be accidental or even hostile to the process of 'being saved.' But the people, thank God, know better than they are taught. The whole Christian message affirms the majesty of the merely human.* *

Yes, community can be difficult. It can be wonderful. And, finally, it is always broader than we think.

3. *Community is always broader than we think*

The gift of the Spirit to *all flesh* (Acts 2:17), and not just to chosen individuals, is a mark of the Messianic age. Somehow Peter knows this, so in his sermon he recalls the words of that mysterious prophet, Joel:

> *And in the last days it shall be, God declares,*
> *That I will pour out my Spirit upon all flesh . . .''* (Acts 2:17/Joel 2:28)

We need to see that the gift of tongues was a gift in the first-century church, but we also need to see that Pentecost was more than just "tongues." Many biblical scholars stress the fact that the

---
*Freedom for Ministry, Richard John Newhaus, Harper & Row, 1979, p. 101.

gift of the Spirit at Pentecost and "speaking in tongues" should be separated, reminding us that at Pentecost we see persons speaking in languages which are known and understood. Communication was at a high level — and at a broad level. In Babel, the peoples' tongues had been garbled (hence, from that time forward, we talk of "babbling"). At Pentecost there was a great reversal of Babel; people came together and had a strong sense of God's presence and direction. It was a great reconciling and outreaching event — a great disciplining of the random, wild tendencies of our sinful human nature.

This narrative is a message to keep us from being so parochial. As I think of my interaction with people as a minister, I know that as soon as we draw lines to keep people out of our community (church), we can be sure that the Spirit is already crossing those lines and moving in the hearts of love. It is a fundamental characteristic of the Spirit that she falls on outsiders as well as insiders. A sign of the future, of tomorrow's will of God, is to be seen wherever outsiders are being welcomed and boundaries of exclusion crossed. Robert Frost, the poet, puts it well in the first four lines of his beautiful piece called "Mending Wall," written over seventy years ago:

> *Something there is that doesn't love a wall,*
> *That sends the frozen-ground-swell under it*
> *And spills the upper boulders in the sun,*
> *And makes gaps even two can pass abreast.* *

Conclusion

The Pentecost event trembles under the weight of supreme significance. It is a mighty act of God, recreated each time we gather for worship. Through these gatherings, our world is alerted to the wonders and works of the Creator of all, whose Spirit broods over and mingles with us all.

**The Poetry of Robert Frost,* Holt, Rinehart and Winston, 1969, p. 33.

Prayer

O God, may your Spirit keep us broken open and vulnerable to hearing the messages you keep sending us through those who have gone before; those around us now; and those whose paths we will one day cross.

The Holy Trinity
Isaiah 6:1-8

Standing in Awe

Introduction

    The really meaningful times in our lives come when we realize how very small — yet cared for and important — we are. As our narrative unfolds today and as his vision emerges for him, Isaiah, the aristrocrat — the prophet — cries out, "Woe is me!" He is stirred to the depths by the experience of the awesome, insurmountable distance between eternal God, the Creator, and the human being, a weak and vulnerable sinner.

    I am lost; for I am a man of unclean lips . . . for my eyes have seen the King, the Lord of hosts! (6:5)

    In the New Testament story of the great catch of fish — when the fish fill the nets so they begin to break and the boat begins to sink — Peter falls down at Jesus' feet and cries, "Depart from me, for I am a sinful man, O Lord." (Luke 5:8) And the experience of Gideon is the same. When the angel of the Lord appears to him, Gideon calls out, "Alas, O Lord God! For now I have seen the angel of the Lord face to face." (Judges 6:22)
    All these people were suddenly and strongly confronted with their vulnerability, humanity and finitude. Their experiences are demonstrations of the way we mortals are drawn to the Creator of our Universe and to our Savior; simultaneously, they demonstrate how we realize our smallness and unworthiness.
    But most of us do not have visions or see angels. Rather we see God in more ordinary ways.

1. The awesomeness of the ordinary

The awesomeness of the ordinary can be just as devastating as the sublime. Let three other voices illustrate:

"I discover the holy not *sub specie aeternitas* (assaulting heaven in all its glory), but by peering under the edges of the ordinary."

— Belden C. Lane*

"The rare moment is not the moment when there is something worth looking at but the moment when we are capable of seeing."

— Joseph Wood Krutch**

"It is when we mistakenly pursue the unusual and sensational in our quest for fulfillment that we rush past the true meaning of life."

— Gerhard Frost***

God is revealed in the small, entrancing surprises of nature. Somewhere Helen Keller says: "Occasionally, if I am very fortunate, I place my hand gently on a small tree and feel the happy quiver of a bird in full song."

And God is revealed, I believe, in the sudden burst of uncontrollable laughter when the sheer surprise of something suddenly hits us. A recent cartoon illustrates it well. It shows an orchestra conductor standing on his podium, looking at the music stand. On that stand is a large hand-lettered note that reads, "Wave the stick until the music stops; then turn around and bow." The fact that my dad was a band leader much of his life made this even more delicious for me. My happiness was such that I found myself wondering, "Why am I allowed this precious moment of joy when I see so many people in my study who need so desperately a small measure of happiness?"

---
*The Christian Century, January 4-11, 1984, p. 15.
**The Desert Year.
***Blessed is the Ordinary, Winston Press, 1980, p. 1.

"Woe is me! for ..."

Yes, God is revealed in the awesomeness of the ordinary. And also in ...

2. *The human drama*

We look, too, to the sensational in human activity to catch a glimpse of the Creator who put all things together. But, once again, that Creator steals in through the smallest of activities. God is so close sometimes that we can't see the presence. For instance, I see the Spirit of God working in the simple imagination of one human being: There was a family who always had trouble on vacations. Each year they would get about seventy-five miles out of town, and Mom would cry, "Oh, no! I left the iron on." Each year they would turn around and go back. But it was never plugged in.

One time the carload was headed for Yellowstone National Park and, sure enough, almost to the mile marker, Mom gasped, "I just know I left the iron on." Her husband didn't say a word. He just pulled over, got out, opened the trunk and hander her the iron. And every year after that, he made sure that the iron was in the trunk before they left on vacation.

We smile at that, but such quiet imagination puts us in awe. We can see God smile too. God is revealed in the drama of humanity as well as in the awesomeness of the ordinary.

While Isaiah has us at it, we can sometimes see God revealed in another way also.

3. *The quiet power of nature*

The voice of God came to Elijah as he was holed up in a cave, not in the strong wind, earthquake or fire, but in "a still small voice." (1 Kings 19:12)

A few years ago, while on a retreat at the Dunrovin Retreat Center, just north of Stillwater, Minnesota, I noticed a banner hanging on the wall with these words, attributed to Peter Marshall:

There is a beauty in homely things which many people have never seen:
- *Sunlight through a jar of peach-plum jelly;*
- *A rainbow in soapsuds in dishwater;*

- *An egg yolk in a blue bowl;*
- *White ruffled curtains sifting moonlight;*
- *The color of cranberry glass;*
- *A little cottage with blue shutters;*
- *Crimson roses in an old stone crock;*
- *The smell of newly baked bread;*
- *Candlelight on old brass;*
- *The soft brown of a cocker's eyes.*

If we read this slowly and reverently, we catch a glimpse, I think, of what Isaiah must have felt when he saw the seraphim and exclaimed,

Holy, holy, holy is the Lord of hosts; the whole earth is full of his glory. (6:3)

Conclusion

The really meaningful times in our lives come when we realize how very small we are — yet cared for and important. The mystery overwhelms us. We see ourselves in Isaiah as he struggles with the mystery and awe of his vision, in the year when King Uzziah died. And a more recent poet helps put it all in perspective for us:

Be patient toward all that is unsolved in your heart. And try to love the questions themselves. Do not seek the answers that cannot be given you because you would not be able to live them. And the point is to live everything. Live the questions now. Perhaps you will then gradually, without noticing it, live along some distant day into the answer.

— *Rainer Maria Rilke*

Prayer

O God, thank you for the sheet wonder of our creation, preservation, and redemption — and for stout promises and bright hopes that keep us thinking kindly of the future.

Proper 4 (May 29 — June 4)
Ordinary Time 9
1 Samuel 16:1-13

God's Choice

Introduction

Samuel knew that Saul's leadership was over. It probably troubled him a great deal to have to anoint a successor. It's never comfortable telling someone they're going to be replaced. But Samuel listened to God speaking to him and followed his strange guidance in selecting a replacement for Saul.

Samuel knew that Saul would not agree to giving up his power. In fact, Saul could probably be counted on to throw one of his famous fits and fly into a murderous rage. So the anointing would have to be in secret. And so it was. The symbolic act only marked out the man who was to be king; he did not become king immediately.

1. It's God's Choice

From start to finish the man who would in due course replace Saul was God's choice. God chose to make the change. He chose the tribe — Judah. He chose the family — Jesse. And he chose the individual. Samuel was only following instructions.

In order to allay suspicion, Samuel took a heifer with him as he went to the house of Jesse, so that it would appear that he was going to Bethlehem for an ordinary sacrifice. Saul was not to know about his impending replacement. Then when he arrived he would invite Jesse and family to the sacrifice — and Yahweh would show him what to do.

"Invite Jesse to the sacrifice, and I will show you what you shall do; and you shall anoint for me him whom I name to you."

— 1 Samuel 16:3

As Jesse's sons pass in review before Samuel, each one in turn is rejected by the Lord — although Samuel would have chosen any one of the first seven he saw. All must have been big, strong, good-looking young men. But God knew the right one had not shown up yet. "Are all your sons here?" asks Samuel. Then comes the dramatic climax to this marvelous story. David is called in from tending the sheep, and Samuel knows when he sees him that he is the one.

And Samuel took the horn of oil, and anointed him in the midst of his brothers; and the Spirit of the Lord came mightily upon David from that day forward.

— 1 Samuel 16:13

A great reign of a great leader was born.

The way we choose people or things is different from how God does it. God chooses us for servanthood, not based on other people's ideas, but rather based on his. Our baptism is God's choice alone (through our parents, to be sure) instead of ours. Remember choosing teams as a youngster? Being first was always a boost for the ego. Even making the team felt good. But our being chosen was always a chancy thing, unless we were a good player. One of my favorite stories is about a little boy who played baseball. He came home from a game one day looking dejected.

"Why the sad look, Rusty?" asked his father. "Lose the game?"

"Nope. It's not that, Dad," he explained. "I gotta play on another team."

"Were you traded?"

"No. Given."

This arbitrary system of small-fry baseball — choosing who will play — must seem like a monster to children who are never "chosen" and merely "left." Thank God we are not chosen for the Kingdom by others, but by God Himself. Because we are part of his family by "God's choice," we can find a measure of peace in our lives.

2. Inward qualities are more important than outward ones

David's eldest brother, Eliab, was a very handsome fellow. But that beautiful verse 7 makes the telling point that inward qualities are more important than outward ones.

The Lord said to Samuel, "Do not look on his appearance or on the height of his stature, because I have rejected him; for the Lord sees not as a man sees; man looks on the outward appearance, but the Lord looks on the heart."
— 1 Samuel 16:7

There's an old saying: "You never get a second chance to make a good first impression." And that's too bad, because first impressions generally do not reveal inward qualities. The anointing of David demonstrates to us that we are to look deeper into each other than to see only what's on the surface.

While a doctor in England was using a small medical light to examine the mouth of a thirty-year-old woman, the bulb and battery became detached from the case and slid gently and painlessly down her throat. In a very real sense the woman suddenly had all the makings of an "inner light."

We smile at that, but there truly is an "inner light" which distinguishes people who are rooted in love and truth. True inner power and light will not shine out easily, but can be observed by listening to our instincts about a person and remembering that "we look on the outward appearance, but the Lord looks on the heart."

Samuel was so in tune with God that he listened to His will in selecting David to be anointed as king. And, arguably, David was Israel's greatest king. This may be an Old Testament counterpart to the principle Jesus expressed when he said,

"Many that are first will be last, and the last first."
Mark 10:31

3. The Spirit is for others

And the Spirit of the Lord came mightily upon David . . .
1 Samuel 16:13

In the Old Testament the function of the Spirit of God is to equip a person with the highest possible ability, whatever might be their task in life. Here David received this Spirit gift, and it was his for keeping until he would need it.

In the Old Testament the Spirit sets people apart from others. In the New Testament the Holy Spirit is given to *all* Christians. In both Testaments, however, the gift of the Spirit is not a possession to be hoarded to oneself with pride, but rather an enabling power for the benefit and service of others. The fact that David was already looking after sheep when Samuel found him was not only literal fact but also symbolically instructive.

I love the story that came out of a major tragedy in one of our states some time back. It demonstrates how heartwarming it is when gifts and possessions are shared with others.

When Alaska experienced a terrible earthquake a couple decades ago, the governor's wife said that she had received many letters and phone calls asking her to help people's relatives and friends. She also received many offers of help. But she received one letter she won't forget. It was from a ten-year-old boy from Bemidji, Minnesota who sent her two nickels. He said he hoped it would help some of the suffering the quake had caused. In a postscript to his letter he had written these words: "P.S. If you need more, please let me know."

Wow! There is sharing at its graceful best! Whether our gift is a couple of nickels or the Holy Spirit, all we do needs to be done with others in mind.

Conclusion

We think we are in charge of our lives (and most of the time we act accordingly). But all that we do — if we listen to the Spirit of the universe — is really by God's choice and permission.

A man's mind plans his way, but the Lord directs his steps.
Proverbs 16:9

That was true for Samuel and David, and it *can* be true for us too.

Prayer

O God, stop our anxious minds from wandering, and our hearts from desiring anything but to know Your will.

Proper 5 (June 5-11)
Ordinary Time 10
1 Samuel 16:14-23

How To Be Used By God

Introduction

David was one of the greatest military commanders and statesmen in history. He established a dynasty that was destined to last for more than four hundred years.

The story of David's early career is interwoven with the events of Saul's reign. (1 Samuel 13:31) His fascinating rise to leadership from the obscurity of a shepherd's life makes for astounding reading. He appeared as a harp player in the king's court. He had a marvelous victory over the giant Goliath and some gallant exploits among the Philistines. After many adventures as the "Robin Hood" leader of a band of outlaws, he was elevated to the rank of King of Israel.

The biblical story was written to glorify the man whose personal charm and charismatic success had made him a popular idol and hero. It has captured the imagination of people in every generation. Indeed, David has been hailed as the greatest of Israel's rulers — "A man after God's own heart."

Through his exploits we can learn something of how to be used by God as we make our pilgrimage through life. His human weaknesses are often pointed out and so he stands, not as an idealized saint in a stained-glass window, but as a flesh-and-blood figure with whom we can identify.

Therefore, our narrative today is not just about this man called David, but it is about each of us. It is an authentic account of what it means to be thrust into leadership — and to accept it.

Our story today suggests at least three ideas about life and leadership. The first thing it points to is:

1. Do not seek high places

If we do the very best job we can on whatever it is we are doing, good things will generally come to us. Truly, we need to plan and set goals. But we also need to concentrate on the task at hand.

David did not seek to be a part of Saul's Court. A "chance" mention of him by one of Saul's servants brought his presence to the fore. David was no ruthlessly ambitious man determined to make his way up the ladder. He was just doing his present task well.

A writer about famous men has this to say about one little-known leader:

> *Charles Crocker was a burly two-hundred-fifty pounder when at the age of twenty-six he left Indiana with a group of young fellows, including two of his brothers, for the trip over the California Trail to the gold fields. He had been born of poor people in Troy, New York, left school at the age of twelve to help support his family, moved to Indiana with his parents, helped clear the land and farm, then worked in a sawmill and an iron forge. Discovering a small deposit of ore, he built a combination blacksmith shop and forge, which he sold in order to provision himself for the westward journey.*
>
> *"I grew up as a sort of leader," says Crocker. "I had always been the one to swim a river and carry a rope across."*
>
> — *Irving Stone*[*]

True leadership will surface. In our narrative today, we see how David's ability was emerging. We need to be patient about progress. If we are thinking too much about tomorrow, today may not be lived as well as it could be. As a student I need to concentrate on studies, not my first parish. Settled in at my first parish, I need to concentrate on that, not dream about the next charge.

---
[*]*Men to Match My Mountains*, Doubleday, 1956, p. 144.

Do not seek high places. If we have done our job, they will come.

Another thought about leadership is the idea that we need to:

2. Prepare well

It may have been David's musical talent that got him the job with King Saul (and later made him famous as the Psalmist), but all the other qualities noted by Saul's servant were royal requisites: David was a man of valor; a man of war; a man prudent in speech; a man of good presence, and the Lord was with him. (1 Samuel 16:18) His training as a shepherd and as a warrior was excellent.

Not only young people, but all of us would do well to continue to study and train for our tasks. "Life-long education" is a word for today. Most vocations require updating of skills and information on a regular basis. And why not learn something new from time to time? Maybe a second language or how to fix your car. Money and time spent for our "heads" are never wasted.

A word of caution, however. It is easy to become professional "preparers" and unconsciously hold back from "getting into things." I read about a young man, starting in college. He vowed he was going to do the best job he possibly could. He bought a large, comfortable chair and placed it in his room. Then he purchased a book-rest which he fastened to the arm of the chair, and also a special study lamp which gave just the right amount of light. After supper he would put on his slippers, adjust the lamp, set up his book rest, place the books in the book rest, and sit down in the big chair. With everything then perfectly adjusted — he would peacefully fall asleep! (From Gerald Kennedy, somewhere.)

We need to prepare well, but dare not get too comfortable in the doing of that preparation.

It's interesting that the one skill which brought David to King Saul's attention was probably a peripheral one — music.

We need to do our present tasks well and not seek higher places. We need to prepare ourselves well. And, finally, in order to be used by God in the way that only we can, we need to:

3. Use our instincts

David is a model for us on this point too. When he met Goliath in battle (1 Samuel 17), he wisely rejected King Saul's armor as not right for him. The offer of bronze helmet and coat of mail was well-intentioned, but to accept it would mean using unfamiliar equipment — equipment that was not made for him. So David chose five smooth stones from the brook, later to be used in his sling. He needed what was authentic to him, even as we need what is authentic to us.

It's a rather long quote, but these words from a theologian/poet speak directly to this concern:

For even though the weaponry urged upon me by my culture in the form of science and knowledge is formidable I cannot work effectively with what is imposed from the outside. Metallic forms hung on my frame will give me, perhaps, an imposing aspect but will not help me do my proper work.

And so I kneel at the brook of scripture, selecting there what God has long been preparing for the work at hand and find smooth stones. The rough edges have been knocked off. The soft parts have been eroded away. They are bare and hard. Nothing superfluous. Nothing decorative. Clean and spare. Scripture has that quality for me — of essentiality, of the necessary. I feel that I am, again, traveling light, delivered from an immense clutter . . .

What strikes me so forcibly . . . is that David was both modest enough and bold enough to reject the suggestion that he do his work inauthentically (by using Saul's armor); and that he was both modest enough and bold enough to use only that which he had been trained to use in his years as a shepherd (his sling and some stones). And he killed the giant.

It is a turning point in the story of God's ways with his people although no one knew it at the time. A new leadership ministry was taking shape. David was not yet king — it would be years before he was recognized as such. He was a marginal figure . . . and slipped back into the obscurity of shepherding in the hill country. The world at that moment seemed divided between the arrogant and bully people of

Philistia and the demoralized and anxious people of God, between the powerful but rather stupid giant and the anointed but deeply flawed king. No one could have guessed that the man picking stones out of the brook was doing the most significant work of the day.

— Eugene H. Peterson*

Conclusion

David didn't engineer his appointment to Saul's court. It seemed, in fact, to happen by mere chance since one of Saul's courtiers knew something about David and brought him to Saul's attention. Yet David was prepared when the call came.

So it was God, not David, who was responsible for this young man's first steps towards the throne as king of Israel. And so it is with us. In our lives, too, it is God who makes and lets things happen.

A person's mind plans his or her ways, but the Lord directs the steps.

— Proverbs 16:9 (Paraphrased for inclusive language)

In times of confusion this is a great comfort.

Prayer

O God, thank you for the critical intervention of
- *the right preparations*
- *the right instincts*
- *the right book*

at precisely the right time.

**Five Smooth Stones for Pastoral Work*, John Knox Press, 1980, pp. 187-188.

Proper 6 (June 12-18)
Ordinary Time 11
2 Samuel 1:1, 17-27

A Royal Lament

Introduction

A bearer of news can be treated especially well, or, as in the case of the Amalekite who brought David the news of the death of Saul and Jonathan, quite badly.

One of David's greatest accomplishments was breaking the Philistines' control over Canaan once and for all and shutting them up in the coastal plain. (2 Samuel 5:17-25; 21:15-22) But at the time described in today's text they were raising havoc with the Israelites — so much so, in fact, that Saul and Jonathan were both killed.

When this news was brought to David, he was sad. A lesser man would have gloated over the death of one who had treated him so badly. But David had a continued respect for the memory of Saul and the office he held. A more ambitious man than David would have been equally pleased about the death of Jonathan, since the young heir would naturally have succeeded to the throne, had he lived.

Instead, David lamented. "He felt no hatred of the man who had pursued him so single-mindedly, nor did he brush him aside like a bad memory. On the contrary, he composed an elegy, a poem to be learned and repeated by the people of Israel, so that the name of Saul, with that of Jonathan, should never be forgotten." (David F. Payne) This marvelous poetry gives fine expression to the best in admiration, vulnerability and friendship.

1. Admiration

David's respect and admiration for leadership and the "office" of King, even though that leadership was flawed, is a fine model for us to study. For all leadership is flawed, and to castigate others in order to build ourselves up never does much good.

An example of this comes from our own day. When James Armstrong was pastor of Broadway Church in Indianapolis (1958-1968), he often preached on America's involvement in the Viet Nam struggle. Patriotic groups often didn't like what he had to say. At a pastors' preaching workshop a few years ago, in North Dakota, I heard him tell about a member of his congregation during that time who differed vehemently with him, but nevertheless respected his leadership and "office." Armstrong told us how that man would stand next to and below the pulpit when he was preaching, open Bible in hand, in silent and respectful disagreement with his pastor on this issue.

Armstrong and that man had many, many conversations about their concerns. Both men loved their church but had differing approaches as to how that church ought to be involved in leadership and witness to the "Good News." One believed the church ought to strive to change peoples' hearts. The other believed the church needs to be involved directly with the events of the day. Both respected each other, so that when Armstrong knew he was going to be having some words about Viet Nam he would alert his friend. Thus would come the silent yet respectful "protest." Only admiration of his pastor (as well as unusual courage) made it possible for such a happening as this.

2. Vulnerability

David's elegy to Saul and Jonathan reveals the vulnerability of our human condition also. In an outburst of hurt David reminds us all of the delicate balance between vigor and stillness, between life and death:

How are the mighty fallen in the midst of the battle! . . .
How are the mighty fallen, and the weapons of war perished!

2 Samuel 1:25, 27

Those of us in our "middle years" know of this vulnerability. We have lived long enough to see all sorts of accidents, illness and just plain surprises. And our bodies grow tired a lot quicker. But our "middle years," given a realistic understanding, can free us up for a recovering of creativity. Ric Masten writes:

I turned forty a while ago and came dribbling out of the locker room ready to start the second half glancing up at the scoreboard I saw that we were behind 7 to 84 and it came to me then we ain't gonna win and considering the score I'm beginning to be damn glad this particular game ain't gonna go on forever

But don't take this to mean I'm ready for the showers take it to mean I'm probably gonna play one helluva second half

I told this to some kids in the court next to mine and they laughed but I don't think they understood how could they playing in the first quarter only one point behind*

We, like David, can recognize our human weakness also.

We have seen that David's elegy speaks of admiration and of vulnerability. It also speaks of . . .

3. Friendship

Except for one verse (26), Jonathan's name is less prominent than Saul's. He, too, was an able soldier, but it was above all his loyal friendship which David recalled and treasured in his memory. The friendship between David and Jonathan has become proverbial, the model of what a friendship should be.

There is a modern model that might also help us get in touch with the importance of friendship. John F. Kennedy, when President of the United States, was often lonely. A man named David was a friend to him. Here is a modern story of a David and Jonathan. The principals in this one are David and John:

Dave was accustomed to being summoned for night duty at

---
*"The Second Half," in *The Deserted Rooster,* Sunflower Ink, 1982.

the White House when Jackie was absent. He called himself "John's Other Wife." The President hated to be alone in the evening. It was understood that Dave would be available to keep him company in the mansion even on nights like this one, when Jackie would be out of the house for only a short time.

During the summer months when Jackie and the children were at Hyannis Port and the President faced solitary confinement in Washington in the evenings from Monday until Thursday, Dave stayed with him until he went to bed. Their nightly routine was always the same. The White House kitchen staff would prepare a dinner of broiled chicken or lamb chops that would be left in the second floor apartment on a hot-plate appliance so that they could eat it late in the evening alone, without keeping any of the staff waiting to serve them. Then they would watch television or sit outside on the Truman balcony, or the President would read a book and smoke a cigar while Dave drank several bottles of his Heineken's beer. "All this Heineken's of mine that you're drinking costs me a lot of money, Dave," the President would say. "I'm going to send you a bill for it one of these days."

Around eleven o'clock, the President would get undressed and slip into the short-length Brooks Brothers sleeping jacket that he wore in preference to pajamas. Dave would watch him kneel beside his bed and say his prayers. Then he would get into bed, and say to Dave, "Goodnight, pal, will you please put out the light?" Dave would put out the light, leave the apartment, say goodnight again to the Secret Service agent on duty in the downstairs hall, and drive home to his own house in McLean, Virginia.

— *Kenneth O'Donnell and David F. Powers**

When Kennedy was assassinated in Dallas on November 22, 1963, Powers was riding in the car just behind him. "Without

---
**Johnny, We Hardly Knew Ye*, Little, Brown, 1972, p. 264.

friends," said Francis Bacon, "the world is but a wilderness." And the Roman poet Cicero wrote, "A true friend is more esteemed than kinfolk." Both of these Davids and Johns seemed to know that.

Conclusion

This elegy/poem is not always easy to understand. It is important to remember that its language is poetic. That helps capture the big picture. It is full of figures of speech and its author never intended it, it seems, to be taken with a wooden literalness.

David has a lot to tell us about relationships. This moving one, between him, Saul and Jonathan (and maybe most relationships), includes admiration, vulnerability and friendship. We can all learn from him here.

Prayer
O God, console the frayed affections of all who
hurt and find it difficult to cope with change.

Proper 7 (June 19-25)
Ordinary Time 12
2 Samuel 5:1-12

The Establishment of An Empire

Introduction

Judged by any standards, the greatest king Israel ever had was David. He seemed destined for leadership even when he was a young boy watching his father's sheep on the rocky Judean hills around Bethlehem. His ascent to Saul's court, his military victories, his capture of Jerusalem — these and other events caused the people from the tribes of Israel to ensconce David as their King. In Israel a man's right to lead was authenticated by divine inspiration. A leader did not hold his position because he came from the right family. It was God who made his imprint on the man. David's rise was great. Taking one step at a time, he gradually grew into full leadership of Israel.

His life was spectacular, but it reflected elements common to all of our lives as well. There was a tentative beginning to his career, a growth through the formative years, and finally an understanding — a perception — of what was happening to and in his existence. It was formulation and a partial answer to the question, "What is life? How do I fit into it?"

1. One Life

Who knows when our career/lives really begin? At 12? 15? 20? For David it seems it was when he was 30 years old.

David was thirty years old when he began to reign, and he reigned forty years. (2 Samuel 5:4)

It was a beginning that would affect the world as nothing else could. A modern writer sums up where this beginning would lead:

He had feet of clay like the rest of us if not more so — self-serving and deceitful, lustful and vain — but . . . you can see why it was David more than anybody else that Israel lost her heart to and why, when Jesus of Nazareth came riding into Jerusalem on his flea-bitten mule a thousand years later, it was as the Son of David that they hailed him. *

We do not know what our lives will become either. Our faith leaves the door open to many mysteries — and their celebration.

And after a beginning, David's career moved along with strength.

And David became greater and greater, for the Lord, the God of hosts, was with him. (2 Samuel 5:10)

There were plenty of setbacks, but the general trend was forward. I suppose that's the way it is with most of us. There are times when it seems that not much is happening in our lives, or even that we are going backward. But generally, if we hang in there, the experience we gain will move us forward. I recall that General Dwight D. Eisenhower, Supreme Commander of the Allied Forces during World War II was a Major in the army for a period of fourteen years. General Eisenhower later became President of our United States of America.

After a beginning, followed by a strong period of growth and leadership, David

. . . perceived that the Lord had established him king over Israel, and that he had exalted his kingdom for the sake of his people Israel. (2 Samuel 5:12)

If we are lucky, and pay attention to our lives, we can often perceive what has happened and how it all fits together. In the case of David, his successes brought more successes and he could see that the Lord, the God of hosts, was with him. Most of us need to

---
*Frederick Buechner, *Peculiar Treasures*, Harper & Row, 1979, p. 24.

listen more in our own lives to what is happening with us. Buechner has some words about this also:

> *God's coming is always unforeseen, I think, and the reason, if I had to guess, is that if he gave us anything much in the way of advance warning, more often than not we would have made ourselves scarce long before he got there.* *

2. Jerusalem

David needed a neutral capital for the united tribes and one that was more central than Hebron. So he and his men took Jerusalem, rebuilt it, strengthened its fortifications, and moved his headquarters there. It was made into the national capital and also the religious capital. Such was the power and appropriateness of this move that even today it stands without rival in Christian affection, not only as the city of David's triumphs but also of Jesus' crucifixion and resurrection. Muslims, too, view it as a holy city, along with Mecca and Medina. David's capture and transformation of Jerusalem changed the world, and the world is the better for it.

As I sit back and reflect on all this I wonder what Jerusalem would have been like today were it not for David. Perhaps it would be like Bennetville:

> *November thirteenth:*
> *Today I passed through Bennetville.*
> *To tell the truth,*
> *I didn't know there was a Bennetville*
> *until today.*
>
> *Passed through,*
> *did I say?*
> *But how can one pass through*
> *a one-store town,*
> *its only dog,*
> *a springer spaniel,*
> *sitting forlornly*
> *in the cold?*

---
*Frederick Buechner, *The Sacred Journey*, Harper & Row, 1982, p. 104.

*I guess I didn't pass through;
I just sped by.*

*I've been thinking:
Why wasn't I born
a Springer spaniel
in Bennetville?*

— Gerhard Frost*

Well, not quite like Bennetville!

3. God will reign supreme

The main point of today's narrative is to point to the stability and security of David and his kingdom. From our view it appears that God's intention was to provide Israel with a period of growth and strength under David's leadership, a golden age which would set the standard for future systems of living. Golden ages are rare in history but they provide goals for us to aim for, ideals to be pursued. In our present age of confusion and change, we can know that the Scriptures and the church have always taught that, ultimately, God is in charge, and that the reign of this Creator will ultimately prevail. Until then we might sing:

Nobody knows the trouble I've seen . . .

. . . but we can also intone:

Glory Hallelujah!

As Christians we can pray, "Thy kingdom come, thy will be done." Yes, cynics and skeptics think about better futures and say, "I'll believe it when I see it." People of faith, however, respond with Saul Alinsky's famous words: "We'll see it when we believe it." Reading this account of David and the Holy City helps a lot.

Conclusion

David and Jerusalem. Quite a story. Because of all this, it came

---
**Blessed is the Ordinary*, Winston Press, 1980, p. 23.

to be believed that God would certainly be in favor of any king who was a son of David. A blind man many years later was to know that too:

> *Bartimaeus, a blind beggar, the son of Timaeus, was sitting by the roadside. And when he heard that it was Jesus of Nazareth [going by], he began to cry out and say, "Jesus, Son of David, have mercy on me!"* (Mark 10:46-47)

Prayer

> *O God, we know that we cannot do everything, or even very much sometimes. But help us to do something.*

Proper 8 (June 26 — July 2)
Ordinary Time 13
2 Samuel 6:1-15

Celebration As Worship

Introduction

After King David had taken Jerusalem, he wished to add to its prestige by making it a religious, as well as a political and military, center. So it was appropriate for him to bring there the ark, the sacred object of the northern tribes, and now the symbol of the national God. He knew that this would help people to acknowledge that Jerusalem was the "dwelling-place" of God.

The sacred symbol had remained under shelter at Kiriath-jearim in the house of Abinadab since the disastrous battles of Samuel's time. So David and his men went to retrieve it and to make its journey to Jerusalem a national affair, as the large numbers of people present indicates. (verse 1)

With this large company of chosen men, David

carried the ark of God upon a new cart, and brought it out of the house of Abinadab which was on the hill . . . And David and all the house of Israel were making merry before the Lord with all their might, with songs and lyres, and harps and tambourines and castanets and cymbals. (2 Samuel 6:3-5)

There is a lot to this story of bringing in the ark. Here are three aspects on which we can focus today: The ark,; Uzzah; and how celebration can be worship.

1. The Ark

As creatures of time and space, we seem to need some sort of center for our faith. The local church serves this purpose for many, and our grand cathedrals attest to this as well. For David and the Israelites the centering impulse was focused on the Ark of the Covenant. One of David's shrewdest acts was to rescue the Ark from the place of oblivion in which it had rested since the fall of the confederate sanctuary of Shiloh, and to bring it to Jerusalem. The contents of the Ark are believed to have been the two tablets of stone on which were recorded the Law (which was considered the basis of the covenant between Yahweh and Israel). It was housed in the Holy of Holies, first in the Tabernacle, later in the Temple. After being kept in a tent-like sanctuary during David's time, it was finally installed in the holiest chamber of Solomon's Temple, beneath the cherubim. Nothing is known of what became of the Ark.

Today in most synagogues an ark is placed in the wall of the structure facing Jerusalem, toward which prayers are directed.

The richness of this symbolism is to be preserved, as is all symbolism that points to our Creator God. But care always needs to be taken that the symbol does not become the main concern. Religion can then become merely form. Halford Luccock tells (somewhere) a story illustrating this:

Once there were some inhabitants of a community in Denmark who, without knowing the origin or purpose of their custom, always bowed to a white wall outside their church when passing in and going out. One day the people began to ask one another why they did that. The mystery was solved, finally, by an historian who found — under the wall's coat of paint — a picture of the Madonna, a painting that had been obliterated at the time of the Reformation. Thus, from habit alone, the people had continued to pay homage to the blank space for twelve generations. We need to be as careful about our history and heritage as were the people of Israel.

2. Uzzah

What a strange narrative this is! When the oxen pulling the ark stumbled, one man instinctively put out his hand to stabilize the precious load. Uzzah had the best intentions, but he died anyway. To lay a casual hand on the sacred ark was considered to be a sacrilege. Holy things must not be handled by anybody except those specially appointed and dedicated as "holy" men.

So strong was this understanding that, conceivably, Uzzah was horrified at his own actions — so much so that he was overcome by fear and suffered a heart attack or something like it. The Old Testament writers saw God's hand in things which we might attribute to natural causes.

God's presence generally means blessing and well-being, but God's power can hurt when we are not careful. The Ark was just a box, physically speaking, and could be carried around quite easily. But it symbolized a God who could not be manipulated or carted around at will. Israel needed to be aware of God's power and anger, just as much as did the Philistines.

Good intentions are not enough. We need to keep the vision clear, the purpose unobstructed. But sometimes we are like the three Girl Scouts who reported to their leader that, as their good deed for the day, they had helped an old woman across the street.

"That's fine," said the Scout leader, "But why did it take three of you?"

"Well," they explained, "she didn't want to go."

We smile at that, but many times our well-meaning acts have been performed because of *our* needs rather than because of the original purpose. Let Uzzah stand for good intentions gone awry.

3. Celebration as Worship

And David and all the house of Israel were making merry before the Lord with all their might. (2 Samuel 6:5)

In the midst of all this joy over bringing the Ark to Jerusalem — amidst all the good feeling of consolidating a people — great happiness was shown.

And David danced before the Lord with all his might . . . So David and all the house of Israel brought up the ark of the Lord with shouting and with the sound of the horn. (2 Samuel 6:14-15)

Such joy and festivity surrounded this journey of the Ark to the capital! We use the phrase "she got carried away" to indicate joyous abandon. That's what David and his people showed here. And that's what little children show in their everyday lives. Didn't Jesus say, "Unless you become as little children . . . "?

A poet/philosopher/caregiver tells us about this in one of his bursts of creative imagination:

> *I want to be ever a child*
> *I want to feel an eternal friendship for the raindrops,*
> *the flowers, the insects, the snow flakes.*
> *I want to be keenly interested in everything,*
> *with mind and muscle ever alert, forgetting my*
> *troubles in the next moment.*
> *The stars and the sea, the ponds and the trees, the*
> *birds and the animals are my comrades.*
> *Though my muscles may stiffen, though my skin*
> *may wrinkle, may I never find myself yawning at life.*
> — Toyohiko Kagawa*

Celebration of life is worship. King David knew how to do that!

Conclusion

We all have our "arks" to remind us of our Creator God. We all can understand Uzzah's instincts. But the mystery of life remains. When we get a glimpse of it, we simply have to dance with all our might. "Dance" as used here, is a generic term. It describes celebration as worship.

Prayer

> *O God, help us to celebrate life, and to live it with*
> *a hop, skip and jump — and with some heavenly*
> *class as well.*

---

*As quoted in *A Running Commentary*, by Roger Prescott, C.S.S. Publishing Company, 1983, p. 21.

Proper 9 (July 3-9)
Ordinary Time 14
2 Samuel 7:1-17

God Dwells With People

Introduction

God had brought the people of Israel out of the bondage of Egypt. Now the Kingdom was being consolidated, even though this God was still dwelling in a tent. The covenant at Sinai (Exodus 19:3-6) molded Israel God's people and their welfare was promised. Long before David there was this promise. Second Samuel 7 relates a new divine promise, one which would make Israel even stronger. The Davidic covenant was God's further promise to provide his people with the leadership they needed. David was the strong beginning; his descendants continued it.

It is good to recall that the New Testament, right from the beginning (Matthew 1), emphasizes that Jesus was the "son of David."

The instructions to David in this narrative were not perfectly clear. He would not be given permission to build a temple, but his offspring would.

> *When your days are fulfilled and you lie down with your fathers, I will raise up your offspring after you, who shall come forth from your body, and I will establish his kingdom. He shall build a house for my name, and I will establish the throne of his kingdom for ever.* (2 Samuel 7:12-13)

God dwells with people wherever they are. And the promises to

David and Israel are promises to us as well. Let the Temple stand for all of our buildings of worship.

They can both hinder and help in our worship of God.

1. Temples and buildings can hinder our worship

We all know how the danger of idolatry encroaches when we get too attached to a building. Yet sometimes we go to the other extreme and say that buildings are not necessary at all for worship. God dwells with his people, wherever they may be. Large and elaborate structures do not "contain" God, though he may be pleased to reveal his presence in them, and they certainly never hinder him. Fine churches, temples or synagogues both help — and hinder — the worship of God. It all depends on how people use such structures.

Every few years there is published in the newspapers the description of a church for which the claim is made that it is the smallest church in the world. One of the most recent in the competition for that title is a church at Upleatham, a little village in North Yorkshire, England. It is a strange little structure, dating back to A.D. 840 and measuring fourteen by seventeen feet. It seats about fifteen persons.

That comes close to being a record for smallness. But if we turn now from our thought of a church as a *building,* and think of it as a *community,* we all know of some pretty small churches. In that respect, the smallest church in the world would be one that shuts out any of God's children. For all are one, and an exclusive church or temple is not large enough to admit the Spirit of God.

God dwells with his people, and large or small structures can hinder our worship. But, conversely, they can also help.

2. Temples and buildings can help our worship

Buildings provide a solidarity to our world. We seem to need a place to focus our energies. The local temple or church building is a place where the "congregation" gathers for worship. And worship can take many forms. It can be the lifting up of our eyes to God through music, architecture, and art, — all of which are tied to buildings most times. Or it can be the mixing of the human family as we gather together to try to find meaning in our existence and order in the topsy-turvy world in which we live. A warm and inviting building can help do that.

That grand old storyteller, Harry Golden, makes this point in one of his stories. When he was young, he once asked his father, "If you don't believe in God, why do you go to the synagogue so regularly?" His father answered, "Jews go to synagogue for all sorts of reasons. My friend Garfinkle, who is Orthodox, goes to talk to God. I go to talk to Garfinkle."

The temple at Jerusalem was to be built in splendor later on, but for now God was interested in establishing another kind of "house." An English word to help clarify this might be "dynasty." So the theme of Nathan's prophecy to David can be expressed in the sentence:

I will not take my steadfast love from him, as I took it from Saul, whom I put away from before you. And your house and your kingdom shall be made sure for ever before me; and your throne shall be established for ever. (2 Samuel 7:15-16)

If temples and buildings can help our worship, they need to be built.

3. High Tech/High Touch

Translating some of this narrative about David — his kingdom, covenant and people — into today's world, I am struck by the fact that our high technology can also either help or hinder our lives.

In John Naisbitt's important book, *Megatrends,* there is a discussion of how the new technology and sophisticated engineering we have developed requires a new emphasis on the human. Where there is "high tech" there needs to be "high touch." There's a beautiful story that illustrates this:

A woman from a small town in North Dakota bought a few stamps each week from the clerk at her post office. In the interest of progress, the government installed a new stamp machine in the lobby one day. The woman never used it but always stood in line to purchase her stamps from the postal clerk. One day he asked her, "Mrs. Johnson, why don't you ever use the machine for stamps? Then you wouldn't have to wait in line."

"Because," she replied quietly, "it never asks about my rheumatism."

We smile at that, but it says much about how important the human touch always is. And God dwells where the people are. The church or synagogue which remains most profoundly aware of its own humanity is closer to the Kingdom of God than the one which is too proud of its buildings and heritage. Buildings and heritage can be nourishing, but they can also get in the way of our remembering that God can raise up "children of Abraham" from stones. Or, as Rev. Jesse Jackson puts it, "Only God can make a way out of no way."

Conclusion

As people of faith we are always "on the way." The story of David and his people is helpful for us to review. David's struggle to consolidate his kingdom, his efforts to establish a base of political and religious strength, and the problems and shortcomings he experiences along the way all remind us of our own pilgrimage through life. People are not perfect. And neither are leaders or dynasties.

Yet, God dwells with people — wherever they are in the pilgrimage of the kingdom. That was the significance of Israel as a chosen people. Temples of brick and stone were not needed by Yahweh, but he could not manifest himself on earth without people.

It was Solomon who built a house for him. Yet the Most High does not dwell in houses made with hands. (Acts 7:47)

The tragedy of the human family is that we are still learning that.

Prayer

O God, thanks for all the architects of our world.

Proper 10 (July 10-16)
Ordinary Time 15
2 Samuel 7:18-29

A Prayer of Wonder

Introduction

David went into the tent which housed the Ark and sat before the Lord. This attitude of devotion seems not to be mentioned elsewhere in the Old Testament, but it is a characteristic posture of prayer in the ancient East. It may be seen in Mohammedan worship to this day.

Both David and his nation were "on a roll." The enemies of the past were crushed (especially the Philistines); the Israelite tribes were uniting and beginning to prosper; and now Jerusalem had become the religious center.

David now ponders it all. This portion of the narrative — 2 Samuel 7:18-29 — is referred to as "David's Prayer." It is a chance to reflect, a chance to pause for thought, a time to sort everything out. Good prayer — nourishing prayer — will do that. All of us need to take time to pause and reflect, to "center ourselves down," and really listen to our lives.

David's prayer is a natural response to the promises that had been made to him and to the success of his kingdom. His prayer includes many things. Here let us speak of three: *humility, praise,* and *acknowledgment.* *

---
*I am indebted to David F. Payne for these thoughts. He speaks of these three responses and two others in his contributions to the *Daily Study Bible Series:* 1 and 2 Samuel — Westminster Press, 1982, pages 191-192.

1. Humility

Then King David went in and sat before the Lord, and said, "Who am I, O Lord God, and what is my house, that thou hast brought me thus far?" (2 Samuel 7:18)

David was feeling good about things and it was a proud time of his life. Grateful humility, not boastful arrogance, was his response to it all. He recognized that it was God who had brought him this far.

In our own prayers humility is needed. But feeling and showing humility are difficult. Our human condition moves us in the direction of thinking it's mostly up to us. Oh, we know that God has created us; "but the important thing is what we do with it." We've all heard the appealing slogan, "If it is to be, it is up to me."

Gerald Kennedy (and others) have told versions of this story:

A rabbi, a cantor, and a humble synagogue cleaner were preparing for the Day of Atonement. The rabbi beat his breast, and said, "I am nothing, I am nothing." The cantor beat his breast, and said, "I am nothing, I am nothing." The cleaner beat his breast, and said, "I am nothing, I am nothing." And the rabbi said to the cantor, "Look who thinks he's nothing."

True humility truly is very difficult! We can sense the depth of authenticity of David's humility in this prayer. Somehow we can sense how it's different from the way we want to be "proud of our humility."

2. Praise

True praise of God is paying attention to all of creation. To know that all is from the hand of this Creator.

O Lord God ... there is none like thee, and there is no God besides thee, according to all that we have heard with our ears. (2 Samuel 7:22)

David could have added all that we have seen with our eyes, too. But sometimes the vast glories of this earth overwhelm us and we lose perspective. True praise is remembering the source and putting first things first.

Seek first his kingdom and his righteousness, and all these things shall be yours as well. (Matthew 6:33)

There was a famous violinist who was asked the secret of her success. She replied: "Well, I used to get up, have breakfast, do the dishes, do the beds, and other minor chores, and *then* I would do my practicing. But I got nowhere. I finally decided to put my practicing first . . . with a program of 'planned neglect' for the other little things which I could do later in the day."

Isn't that great? Isn't that fine! "Planned neglect!" Perhaps that's another word for praise of God.

During this time of introspection David was putting things back in perspective and realizing that Yahweh — the Lord — was to be remembered always and to be put first in praise and thanksgiving.

For the moment everything was going well for David. His enemies had been overcome and none of the great world powers of the future had yet risen. David's word was listened to throughout a wide empire inhabited by many people. Even though this success would bring danger and temptation later on, for now, at least, all was well. And David gave praise and thanks to the Source of it all.

3. *Acknowledgment*

Praying itself is an acknowledgment, a realization that there is Someone beyond ourselves that has caused all things to be.

And now, O Lord God, thou art God, and thy words are true, and thou hast promised this good thing to thy servant; now therefore may it please thee to bless the house of thy servant, that it may continue for ever before thee; for thou, O Lord, hast spoken, and with thy blessing shall the house of thy servant be blessed for ever. (2 Samuel 7:28-29)

Children have a natural knack for acknowledging God. A young boy who had done something bad was told by his mother that he could not go to a picnic that had been planned for the next weekend. But when the day came she was sorry for him and told him that he could go. He seemed quite indifferent. She asked him, "Don't you want to go?" He replied, "I'm sorry, but I have already prayed for rain."

Such simple faith makes us smile a little, but perhaps this kind of acknowledgment is closer to the truth than our vapid utterings.

In this prayer of David (especially verses 25-29) we see great acknowledgment that God had given what he promised and that he would indeed keep all of his promises for the future. The main purpose of these verses may well have been for later generations to read, in times when the blessings in verse 29 seemed rather dim.

Humility, praise and acknowledgment. Three great responses to what God has done for us all. The next time you pray, why not try doing all three?

Conclusion

The key to understanding this chapter is the play on the various meanings of the word *house*. According to the footnotes in my Oxford annotated Bible . . .

- in vv. 1-2 it means "palace."
- in vv. 5, 6, 7, 13 it means "temple."
- in vv. 11, 16, 19, 25, 26, 27, 29 it means "dynasty."
- and in v. 18 it means "family status."

It was in terms of all these meaningful things that David prayed. He has left us a marvelous legacy of a model prayer. Perhaps only the Lord's Prayer (Matthew 6) and Jesus' High Priestly Prayer (John 17) are on the same plane with this prayer of David.

Prayer

> *O God, when confronted by mystery, help us to remember that we do not have to explain all we we know or understand or believe.*

Proper 11 (July 17-23)
Ordinary Time 16
2 Samuel 11:1-15

Feet Of Clay

Introduction

King David was riding a crest. He had broken the Philistines' control over Canaan once and for all. He had captured the old fortress of Jerusalem, despite the boast of its occupants that it was impregnable. He had rescued the Ark of the Covenant from the place of oblivion in which it had rested since the fall of the confederate sanctuary of Shiloh, and had brought it to Jerusalem. He had begun to consolidate the Israelite nation. He was a leader, and he was loved. He seemed to be able to do anything he wanted.

Yet at the very heart of this success lurked danger. Could he wield his great power without being corrupted by it? Would success go to his head, convincing him that he could have anything he wanted? Listen to how one theologian/poet tells what happens next:

> *He ... remembered the first time he had ever seen her. The latest round of warfare with the Syrians had just ended, and his victory had left him feeling let down. He drank too much at lunch and went upstairs for a long nap afterwards. It was almost twilight when he awoke. The palace was unusually quiet, and he felt unusually solemn and quiet inside his own skin. There were no servants around for some reason, nobody to remind him that he was anointed king, victorious general, all that. He bathed, made himself a drink, and with just a towel wrapped around his waist, walked out onto the*

terrace on the roof where he looked down over the parapet in a kind of trance.

If the whole Syrian army had been drawn up in battle dress, he would have simply noted their presence and passed on. There was a bay gelding tethered to a tree, sweeping the flies away with his tail. In the servants' court, a cistern had overflowed onto the cobbles, leaving a puddle the shape of Asia. Beyond a wall, a naked girl stood in a shallow pool dipping water over her shoulders with a shell. In as detached a way as he saw the girl, he saw both that he had to have her at any cost and that the cost would be exorbitant. Her husband's murder, the death of their first child — like actors awaiting their cues, the fatal consequences lurked just out of sight in the wings. *

David was human after all, and his leadership took a new turn. What happened to him and Bathsheba happens to us all in one way or another. First we are overcome with temptation. Then we get in deeper. And finally we discover the God's grace is big enough for anything.

1. Overcome with temptation

By now David thought he could do anything. Certainly he knew it was wrong to take another man's wife but he had convinced himself that he was outside the usual laws. The clean, sparse words of Scripture describe the moment:

So David sent messengers, and took her. (2 Samuel 11:4)

Men and women today, caught up in the hurts and pressures of their lives, often succumb to the temptation to disregard their marriage vows and carry on flirtatious exchanges. When that happens we all need to be reminded of the words of Luther:

You can't keep the birds from flying over your head, but you can keep them from building nests in your hair.

---

*Frederick Buechner, *Peculiar Treasurers,* Harper & Row, 1979, pp. 15-16.

David was headed for a fall because he forgot that he was subject to universal codes of conduct as was everyone else. And the fall, though temporary, was great. And it had a lasting effect on him and many other people. Uriah would die, as would his first child. Perhaps a modern ditty could sum it up for us. Going against tried and true guidelines can turn things sour:

The glances over cocktails
that seemed to be so sweet
do not seem quite so amorous
over breakfast shredded wheat.

— Benny Fields

Our narrative began like this:

In the spring of the year, the time when kings go forth to battle . . . (2 Samuel 11:1)

It was also the time when romance was in the air.

2. Getting in deeper

To cover up the scandal, the king sent for Uriah, who was Bathsheba's husband and one of David's army commanders serving under Joab. David hoped to make it seem that Uriah was the father of Bathsheba's unborn child. But the plan didn't succeed. Uriah refused to break the strict rules of a consecrated soldier in holy warfare and would not visit his wife. This loyal soldier believed that by visiting and sleeping with his wife he would betray his hard-pressed comrades-in-arms as they did battle.

When Uriah asked to return to the battlefield, David sent a message, by the hand of Uriah himself, to Joab in which he instructed his general

Set Uriah in the forefront of the hardest fighting, and then draw back from him, that he may be struck down and die.
(2 Samuel 11:15)

As Sir Walter Scott said, "Oh what a tangled web we weave, when first we practive to deceive." (*Marmion,* 1808) This kind of activity by David rings a bell with all of us — if we look carefully at ourselves.

Adultery and murder: some pretty heinous crimes. Yet we know from later accounts that David would recover, be forgiven and live to serve God in further ways. God's grace is big enough for anything. That promise brings hope, comfort and new beginnings to us all.

3. God's grace is big enough for anything

From this side of the Resurrection, we people of the Christian faith know of God's grace through Jesus Christ. That Grace was at work in David's day too, but it is clearer for us now. The circle has been made whole — from David through the Son of David through you and me. God's grace has continually to be re-examined and perceived through "new eyes." Here is a story Dennis Benson has shared in his book *Making Tracks*. It helps put "Grace" in a broader light. (Abingdon, 1979, pp. 32-34.) It comes from the Eskimo culture:

I was about sixteen. My father, two men, and I were fishing on the edge of the ice. One kayak was tied to the ice. The water was open. The piece of ice on which we were standing broke off, and very quickly we were pulled out into the Arctic by the currents. Along with wind and weather, it was a very serious situation.

I remember my father's looking at us and saying, "Don't panic, or we die." He proceeded to get into the one kayak that was tied to the ice, and I expected to go along with my father because I often rode two in the boat. But my father looked at me and said, "Sam, you stay here." Of course, I didn't argue with my father, but I wondered why he would leave me out there instead of taking me back to safety with him.

My father did make it back to the village. Some people had seen the ice break off and had rung the bell.

A group of men had brought down some other kayaks. My father tied on three other boats behind him and found his way back to the ice floe. I can remember Father's coming up to the ice, and the water that splashed on him froze solid on his body. The only place it hadn't frozen was on his hands because he was pulling the double-bladed paddle . . .

When we had made it back to the village, I asked my father why he had left me out there. "Why didn't you let me go back with you the first time?" My father looked at me and said, "Sam, I looked at the other two men, and I was afraid they would panic and die. I knew that if I left my only son there, they would know that I would be back."

Conclusion

King David had feet of clay — just as do we all. After committing adultery he got in trouble deeper by trying to cover it up with a murder. But such is the grace of God that from David's seed was to come the Messiah — Jesus the Christ, the Son of God. Because God sent his only Son to earth, we know that he has been with us — and will be again.

Prayer

O God, guide us back from the brinks of our temptations and give us a freshness of spirit to renew our faith and brighten our hopes.

Proper 12 (July 24-30)
Ordinary Time 17
2 Samuel 12:1-14

The Promise Of Life
("U" Turns Permitted)

Introduction

King David had risen to power and put together many good things. But power went to his head and he succumbed to adultery and murder. After Bathsheba had dutifully gone through mourning ceremonies for Uriah, her slain husband, David brought her to his house. She became his wife and bore him a son. Business as usual. Would no one dare raise a voice in protest against the king for taking Uriah's wife and life — would they?

Many times kings and national leaders are able to "get away with" their misdeeds. Was David above the law? Was President Nixon above the law in the Watergate episode? No matter what human governments might do, God is the final judge.

> *The thing that David had done displeased the Lord.* (2 Samuel 11:27)

So something surprising happened — an amazing event that would not have taken place in any other Oriental nation, of that time or later. With matchless courage, Nathan the prophet confronted King David. Thus, the most famous parable in the Old Testament was told.

1. Getting off the track

King David had gone too far — had gotten off the track.

Someone needed to bring him up short. But how? A king was beyond judging by ordinary people. Nathan, believing that he had a commission from God, had the courage to challenge the king to his face. It's something a true friend might do today.

Nathan told King David a story about two men, ostensibly because he wanted the king's advice in the matter. One of the men was wealthy and had many lambs. The other was poor, owning only one ewe lamb that was a household pet for the man's children. The poor man loved this lamb as one of his children. Yet one day the wealthy man decided to take that poor man's ewe lamb, even though he himself had many.

David's response to this tale was what Nathan had hoped for. He renounced the rich man and gave his royal opinion angrily:

As the Lord lives, the man who has done this deserves to die; and he shall restore the lamb fourfold, because he did this thing, and because he had no pity. (2 Samuel 12:5-6)

Then follows one of the most dramatic moments recorded in Scripture. The prophet advanced, pointed to David, and said, "You are the man." (2 Samuel 12:7)

David, even though a king, had gotten off the track and needed a special kind of confrontation to see it.

A leader, especially, needs to set a positive model for others. A man was stranded by one of our unpredictable North Dakota blizzards. Against the advice of everybody who knew the conditions of the roads, he decided to start out for home the next day. It took him over four hours to go a distance which normally he could have made in less than an hour. There were huge drifts of snow and the wind was blowing so hard that visibility was almost zero. There was ice covering the highway and to make matters worse, his windshield wipers had broken. Finally he could go no farther. He stopped and just sat for a while in his marooned car, wondering what to do.

Much to his surprise, someone tapped at his window. "I have been following you for the last several miles," the stranger began. "They told me in town that I couldn't get through, but I saw you go, so I thought I would try it, too."

If we are leaders (and we all are, in one way or another) we need to think carefully in our decisions so that we do not lead people astray into situations that might harm them — or others. Not all of us are "lucky" enough to have a Nathan.

2. *It is always easier to see other people's faults*

Nathan's parable was powerful in its effect because it first disarmed the king. David was sure this was a story about "Somebody else's" incident. And it is always easier to see other people's faults. Centuries later Jesus would echo the gist of this encounter when he said

> *Why do you see the speck that is in your brother's eye, but do not notice the log that is in your own?* (Matthew 7:3)

There was once a woman who was highly critical of her neighbors. Nothing they did was ever "right;" and she told everyone about how poorly they reared their children, kept their yards, and did their work. One day a visitor was being regaled with these complaints; and the woman, looking out of her window, said, "There's an example of what I mean. Look at the dirty wash on her line. The sheets are streaked with dirt." The visitor went over to look out the window and then raised it. "My dear," she said gently, "the dirt streaks are on your windows."

Why is it so easy for us to see the shortcomings of others? In this case, Nathan used David's human nature to advantage.

3. *"U" turns permitted*

Lots and lots of signs on roadways warn us "No U Turn." But in this adventure called life, we need to have permission to make many "U" turns. Nathan had given David an opportunity to do just that. After Nathan had voiced those devastating words, "You are the man," David said to Nathan — in words that reveal a deep sense of guilt and penitence — "I have sinned against the Lord." (2 Samuel 12:13)

Usually we don't get "lost" or "off the track" all at once. More often, we do as sheep do: we sort of "nibble ourselves lost." When we finally realize how far we have gone astray, if we're lucky we'll admit it and make an immediate turn around. A "U" turn. And in all cases it is we who have drifted away, not God.

A couple, celebrating their 25th wedding anniversary, were taking a trip to Minneapolis. On the freeway they suddenly found themselves behind an old clunk of a car in which a young man and a young woman were sitting very close together, obviously much in love.

"Why don't we ever sit that way any more, dear?" said Eloise to her husband.

Continuing to look straight ahead, Walter quietly said, "I haven't moved."

We smile at that, but there's a lot of truth to it. When relationships have changed — when we have lost sight of our original principles — then it is time to make a "U" turn. David did that, and somewhat redeemed himself in our eyes — and in God's.

Conclusion

In this famous narrative of Nathan and David we see revealed the axiom that a "parable" — a "story" — can be truer than an actual event, with its facts and dates. Not only does this parable of Nathan turn a king around, but it reveals one of the powerful ways in which the Bible speaks. By "stories," some true and some made up, God speaks to us through the human drama of life. I still remember those (at first) puzzling words of Karl Barth: "I take the Bible too seriously to take it literally."

And Nathan said to David, "The Lord also has put away your sin; you shall not die." (2 Samuel 13)

By these words of Nathan's, David saw with new eyes. He received a promise of life. We have that promise too.

Prayer

O God, thank you for the dead-end streets and "U" turns made — and the open roads that follow.

Proper 13 (July 31 — August 6)
Ordinary Time 18
2 Samuel 12:15b-24

Back in the Swing

Introduction

Because the David story ascends the height of human aspiration and plumbs the depths of human anguish, it has outlived the political circumstances from which it came. The prophet Nathan's final prediction was to come true. David and Bathsheba's son, conceived out of wedlock, died in infancy. It is clear that the child was very precious to David. It became sick, and . . .

> *David therefore besought God for the child; and David fasted, and went in and lay all night upon the ground.*
> (2 Samuel 12:16)

It is obvious that the boy's death was a punishment for David. According to the idea of the *lex talionis* (law of exact retaliation, Exodus 21:23; Leviticus 24:19-21; Deuteronomy 19:21), David should have died. Instead, divine judgment fell upon the child, according to the ideas of that day, as a special favor to David. It could have been worse.

In this narrative we have a tragic death; a movement back into the routine of life; and a new life — a new promise of hope.

1. A tragic death

It always hurts when a child dies. Even in this case, when David expected it — and knew he deserved it — it hurt deeply. He hurt so much when he knew his first child was going to die that he cast himself upon the ground, and . . .

> *The elders of his house stood beside him, to raise him from the ground; but he would not, nor did he eat food with them.* (2 Samuel 12:17)

I remember the night my sister called and said that Mom was dying. She had fallen at her Health Care Center, probably due to a stroke. The outlook was not good. Our prayers were not that she should be miraculously healed, but that she might not suffer too much. She died the next morning and a marvelous peace came over me. The burial at the cemetery, when only her three children and her son-in-law were present, mirrored this peace. I recall the many times I said to my congregation, "The peace of God which passes all understanding, keep your hearts and your minds in Christ Jesus." The "Peace of God" was with us that day. I wrote this about it:

> *Grandview Cemetery. Aptly named. High on a hilltop, just outside Fayette, Iowa. January 26, 1984. 31 degrees. A gentle winter day. The snow-filled arms of the evergreens surround us as we pay a final tribute to our Mom. Marge, Jer, Neb, and I take turns reading — "In sure and certain hope of the resurrection to eternal life . . . we commend to almighty God our Mother, Elsie . . . earth to earth, ashes to ashes . . . " She was born and grew up only a mile from here, and there is a comfort to this place and to this day. Elsie Mae Fussell Prescott has finally stepped beyond the boundaries of her life, and her troubles are gone now. She has come to the true ease of herself. So long, Mom. We love you. We'll miss you. May your memory be blessed forever.*

Death is always real. And it hurts. But sometimes, also, it brings a peace. That's what seemed to happen to King David.

> *Then David arose from the earth, and washed, and anointed himself, and changed his clothes; and he went into the house of the Lord, and worshiped.* (2 Samuel 12:20)

2. Back in the swing

When David and Bathsheba's young son became fatally ill, David fasted and prayed. But after the child died, David, a realist, anointed himself, changed clothes, ate a little bit, worshiped, and even had sex with his wife. (2 Samuel 12:20, 24)

This seems wise. In dealing with grief, sometimes it's good to get back into doing the same things one did before the illness and death. It is wise counsel to urge people not to make any major changes for a while after a death. Getting back into the swing of the old routine can do wonders. As the late psychotherapist Karen Horney said:

Life itself remains a very effective therapy.

And Rabbi Abraham Heschel:

Just to be is a blessing. Just to live is Holy.

Buechner knows the value and holiness of the everyday routine, and he puts it in marvelous prose:

One holy place I know is a workshop attached to a barn. There is a woodburning stove in it made out of an oil drum. There is a workbench, dark and dented, with shallow, crammed drawers behind one of which a cat lives. There is a girlie calendar on the wall, plus various lengths of chain and rope, shovels and rakes of different sizes and shapes, some worn-out jackets and caps on pegs, an electric clock that doesn't keep time. On the workbench are two small plug-in radios, both of which have serious things wrong with them. There are several metal boxes full of wrenches, and a bench saw. There are a couple of chairs with rungs misssing. There is an old yellow bulldozer with its tracks caked with mud parked against one wall. The place smells mainly of engine oil and smoke — both wood smoke and pipe smoke. The windows are small, even on bright days what light there is comes through mainly in window-sized patches on the floor.

I have no idea why this place is holy, but you can tell it is the moment you set foot in it if you have an eye for that kind of thing.*

— Frederick Buechner

David returned to his everyday world. It is the world where God is present in the ordinary — which is the holy. That's not a bad plan for all of us. Perhaps it is true that the ordinary makes the unendurable endurable.

3. A new life

Perhaps the most important part of this narrative is verse 24:

Then David comforted his wife, Bathsheba, and went in to her, and lay with her; and she bore a son, and he called his name Solomon. And the Lord loved him. (2 Samuel 12:24)

This child was the son destined to be David's successor but no reason is ever given why Solomon, rather than one of his brothers, should have been marked out to succeed David. Indeed, we are surprised. We might have expected that the union between Bathsheba and David, based as it was on murder and adultery, would never be blessed. We stand awed by the mystery of the grace of God. God can, truly, carve tunnels of hope in mountains of despair. He can bring life out of death, a happy and courageous spirit out of a tragic event.

In 1955 Mary Alyce Knudson, mother of three, was struck down by polio shortly before the Salk vaccine was developed. Since then she has been a quadriplegic, confined to a wheelchair, with only limited use of her left hand. From her home in Fargo, North Dakota, Mary Alyce has raised her boys, been a companion to her husband, and trained her left hand to write and draw. Beautiful cards called "Mary's Moments" and a book on Troll Legends has been published by this remarkable woman. But the most amazing thing of all is her "upbeat" spirit. She is a joy to be around and always raises the hopes of all she meets. Out of her tragedy has come a new life, and in 1982 she was voted North Dakota's Outstanding Handicapped Citizen of the year. She doesn't waste her time asking, "Why did this happen to me?" She rather has asked

---
*Wishful Thinking, Harper & Row, 1973, p. 39.

by her life itself, "What do I do now with what I have?" She is living the depth of our Christian faith, and, along with King David, is a model for us as we see that "God can make a way out of no way."

Conclusion

Perhaps the words of an Eighteenth-Century hymn can best sum up this sermon on death and life:

God moves in a mysterious way,
   His wonders to perform;
He plants his footsteps
   in the sea
And rides upon the storm.

Judge not the Lord
   by feeble sense,
But trust him
   for his grace;
Behind a frowning
   providence
Faith sees a smiling face.

LBW 483, Stanzas 1 and 2
By William Cowper (1731-1800)

Prayer

O God, make us willing now, so that things of eternal significance may begin to happen here.

Proper 14 (August 7-13)
Ordinary Time 19
2 Samuel 18:1, 5, 9-15

Human Nature Revisited

Introduction

In this moving narrative we have several very effective character studies: King David, torn between losing a battle and losing his son; Absalom, the ambitious young man, caught by the "chances" of life; and "a certain man", a soldier of Joab's, caught between loyalty to his King and loyalty to his commander.

As parents, as leaders, as citizens of our country, we can all identify with the age-old dilemmas played out so powerfully in this account. When we look at the human situations described in this narrative, and then look into our own hearts, we can truly see "human nature revisited." The mysteries of human nature are the same as they were three thousand years ago (and probably will be three thousand and and more years from now).

1. A parent's dilemma

On the eve of a crucial battle, David was a wreck. He wanted to be in the battle but he also knew that if he was killed, the mantle of leadership would flounder. (See 2 Samuel 21:17) So he let his commanders talk him into staying back. But he was afraid for his son. While Absalom had cast away every shred of loyalty to his father and was prepared to bring about his father's death in order to expand his own ambitious ends, David thought only of his son, to the exclusion of his own — and his country's — interests. So the King said to his commanders:

Deal gently for my sake with the young man Absalom.
(2 Samuel 18:5)

Such tender and difficult words! Hasn't every parent been torn between helping their children and letting matters take their course? One of our contemporary writers has captured this dilemma beautifully — mysteriously echoing the relationship between David and Absalom:

I see my son is wearing long trousers, I tremble at this;
I see he goes forward confidently, he does not know so fully his own gentleness.
Go forward, eager and reverent child, see here I begin to take my hands away from you,
I shall see you walk careless on the edges of the precipice, but if you wish you shall hear no word come out of me;
My whole soul will be sick with apprehension, but I shall not disobey you.
Life sees you coming, she sees you come with assurance towards her,
She lies in wait for you, she cannot but hurt you;
Go forward, go forward, I hold the bandages and ointments ready,
And if you would go elsewhere and lie alone with your wounds, why I shall not intrude upon you,
If you would seek the help of some other person, I shall not come forcing myself upon you.
If you should fall into sin, innocent one, that is the way of this pilgrimage;
Struggle against it, not for one fraction of a moment concede its dominion.
It will occasion you grief and sorrow, it will torment you.
But hate not God, nor turn from Him in shame or self-reproach;
He has seen many such, His compassion is as great as His Creation.
Be tempted and fall and return, return and be tempted and fall
A thousand times and a thousand, even to a thousand thousand.

> *For out of this tribulation there comes a peace, deep in the soul and surer than any dream . . .*
>
> — Alan Paton*

Our children bring out mixed emotions in us all. For David, Absalom was a thorn in his flesh, but he was also the apple of his eye.

2. The "chances" of life

David wasn't the only one in the narrative struggling with a dilemma. Absalom, too, was left hanging — literally. I like the way the Bible writer says

> *And Absalom chanced to meet the servants of David.*
>
> (2 Samuel 18:9)

In the forest of Ephraim a battle was fought between David's loyal men and Absalom's rebels. Riding through the forest on his mule, Absalom was caught (maybe by his long hair) in the branches of a great oak tree. He was left helplessly hanging when his mule ran out from under him. David's commander Joab found him in this situation and slew the young traitor, knowing that an enemy of the king surely had to die, even if he was the king's own son.

Over and over again we, too, are caught unawares because we have not foreseen the incidental and "chance" character of the battlegrounds of life. I think of that great prayer in the Compline service of the Lutheran Book of Worship:

> *Be present, merciful God, and protect us through the hours of this night, so that we who are wearied by the changes* and chances *of life may find rest in you; through Jesus Christ our Lord. AMEN* (LBW, p. 157)

And that surprising Proverb:

> *A man's mind plans his way, but the Lord directs his steps.*
>
> (Proverbs 16:9)

---

*"Meditations for a Young Boy Confirmed" The Christian Century, 13 Oct. 1954

Lest we think that all in this world is "cause and effect," we need to hear from a contemporary theologian/rabbi who writes about the "unfair distribution of suffering in the world."

> *There is only one question which really matters: why do bad things happen to good people? All other theological conversation is intellectually diverting; somewhat like doing the crossword puzzle in the Sunday paper and feeling very satisfied when you have made the words fit; but ultimately without the capacity to reach people where they really care. Virtually every meaningful conversation I have ever had with people on the subject of God and religion has either started with this question, or gotten around to it before long. Not only the troubled man or woman who has just come from a discouraging diagnosis at the doctor's office, but the college student who tells me that he has decided there is no God, or the total stranger who comes up to me at a party just when I am ready to ask the hostess for my coat, and says, "I hear you're a rabbi; how can you believe that . . . " — they all have one thing in common. They are all troubled by the unfair distribution of suffering in the world.*
>
> — Harold S. Kushner[*]

I guess Absalom would have agreed. On the other hand, there is also an unfair distribution of good fortune and the "chances" of life can lift us up too. An unplanned-for monetary success or perhaps an inheritance can smooth the edges, take away the insecurities, and let the nice things of life come out. Listen to one of the grand nature writer/philosophers of our day. She writes of a summer home and what it has meant to her:

> *If I were a wise woman, I should understand many things about life which I do not now understand. Maybe I would know why there is so much evil walking the highways, why (we) must suffer, why the governments operate like kaleidoscopes instead of like good blueprints for living, why gentle people must die too soon.*

---
[*]*When Bad Things Happen to Good People,* Schocken Books, 1981, p. 6.

> *I think about all these things, up in the old orchard with Holly's muzzle soft in my hand. And about the first people who owned Stillmeadow's forty acres more or less. What dreams they had of a fair world with liberty and justice for all.*
>
> *And suddenly I know. I know there is a dream that will not die, and that Stillmeadow, in a small and quiet way, is an affirmation of that dream.*
>
> — Gladys Taber*

For some, the grace of "chances" improves our lot. For Absalom the "chances" did him in.

3. Idealism of Realism?

The warrior who here explains his refusal to kill Absalom (2 Samuel 18:12-13) was possessed of a remarkable combination of loyalty and common sense — of idealism and realism. He had heard the king's command to deal gently with the young man Absalom; he also knew the character of his commanding officer, Joab. Happy is the one who knows both the faithfulness of God and the untrustworthy character of friends who urge disobedience. This "certain man," a "private first class" perhaps in Joab's army, was an idealist and a realist at the same time. He was an idealist in that the King's word was meant to be faithfully obeyed; he was a realist in his appreciation of what Joab's promise was worth. Perhaps something like this was intended when Jesus said

> *So be wise as serpents and as innocent as doves.*
> (Matthew 10:16)

This unusual combination of idealism and realism is beautifully demonstrated in one of my favorite stories. Senator Jacob Javits likes to tell about a neighbor's little daughter who really believes in the power of prayer. But she is a realist also. When her brother built a trap to catch sparrows, she prayed hard that he wouldn't catch any. He didn't.

The Best of Stillmeadow, J. B. Lippincott, 1976, p. 348.

Some days later her father asked, "What made you so sure your prayer would be answered?" "Well, for one thing, Father," replied the devout and idealistic youngster, "I went back there three days ago and kicked the trap to pieces."

Beautiful! In this case some sparrows were saved. In the case of the "private" in Joab's army, he managed to save his neck too. A healthy mixture of idealism and realism will stand us in good stead. The art is in finding the proper balance.

Conclusion

Life's dilemmas are real. We can take heart by knowing that they have been — and probably will be — with us forever. To know that we are like others can "soften the blows" of life.

Prayer

O God, we are wearied by the changes and chances of life. Help us to pause in our feverish activities and listen to what you have to say.

Proper 15 (August 14-20)
Ordinary Time 20
2 Samuel 18:24-33

A Grief Observed

Introduction

When King David learned that yet another of his sons had died, even though he had been a rebellious and unloyal one, it broke his heart. He could not be comforted with the thought that he had regained his kingdom. All he could do was to cry in his broken anguish

> *"O my son Absalom, my son, my son Absalom! Would I had died instead of you, O Absalom, my son, my son!"*
> (2 Samuel 18:33)

These words have echoed down the centuries ever since they were uttered and they are one of the most distressing scenes in all literature. David's deep anguish arises not only out of the death of his son, but out of his own failure as a father. Many a father in today's world can identify with this. Successful in our own vocations and work world, we find it more difficult to be a "successful" parent.

"O my son Absalom!" This heartbreaking cry — this grief observed — points out several things we need to know. (1) It makes clear that the Bible can be read for its human drama; (2) it reminds us that it's okay to cry; and (3) it reveals the agony of knowing what might have been.

1. The Bible as human drama

The Bible does not play down the deep reality of human emotions. All of its characters behave almost too humanly. The loss of yet another well-loved son was a matter of almost unbearable sorrow for David. And in this sorrow we see how he shares common humanity with all the rest of us.

From the parting of the waters of the Red Sea . . .

Then Moses stretched out his hand over the sea; and the Lord drove the sea back by a strong east wind all night, and made the sea dry land, and the waters were divided.
(Genesis 14:21)

. . . to the return of the Prodigal Son . . .

"Bring quickly the best robe, and put it on him; and put a ring on his hand, and shoes on his feet . . . for this my son was dead, and is alive again . . . "
(Luke 15:22-24)

. . . to Nathan's piercing words to David . . .

"You are the man." (2 Samuel 12:7)

The Scripture is filled with as high and dramatic moments as could ever be known.

And now King David emotes his most plaintiff cry . . .

"O my son Absalom, my son, my son Absalom!"
(2 Samuel 18:33)

Dramatic, powerful stuff, all this. In one sense David was a victim of his own greatness, of a strong will that urged him to scale the tempting heights of power. Yet, in spite of his drive for success and national glory, he was never lacking in the magnanimity and winsomeness that made both friend and foe love and respect him simultaneously.

It seems significant that tradition has ascribed to David the great confessional prayer, Psalm 51. The words there speak of deep human anguish and penitence:

> *Have mercy on me, O God,*
> *   according to thy steadfast love . . .*
> *Purge me with hyssop, and I shall be*
> *   clean . . .*
> *Fill me with joy and gladness;*
> *   let the bones which thou hast*
> *   broken rejoice.*
> *Hide thy face from my sins,*
> *   and blot out all my iniquities.*
> *Create in me a clean heart, O God,*
> *   and put a new and right spirit*
> *   within me.* (Psalm 51:1, 6, 8-10)

The Bible could be read with profit even if only for the high drama contained within it.

2. It's okay to cry

Jesus wept over the city of Jerusalem (Luke 19:41) and over his friend Lazarus. (John 11:35) No doubt he wept on many other occasions also. Somehow we have gotten the idea, however, that "big boys don't cry." That notion needs to be changed, and the Bible gives us permission to cry when we hurt. If Jesus wept often and Abraham Lincoln was seen with tears streaming down his face, and a presidential candidate (Edmund Muskie) can openly cry, why do we not allow ourselves to do so? We do not show openness to others by excluding them from our pain. As Charles Dickens has Mr. Bumble say in *Oliver Twist,*

> *Crying opens the lungs, washes the countenance, exercises the eyes, and softens down the temper, so cry away.*

Perhaps no one could have used the words with such understanding as David when he said:

> *Weeping may tarry for the night, but joy comes with the morning.* (Psalm 30:5)

Absalom's death had gained David entrance to the largest company of people in the world — those who have suffered pain.

3. What might have been

"O my son Absalom, my son, my son Absalom!"

As I read these words and they sear their way into my soul, I recall another father, saddened by the tragic death of his son. Dr. Alvin Rogness, former President of Luther Seminary in St. Paul, Minnesota, had a son, Paul, whose life was snuffed out at age twenty-four, on a city street ten minutes from the family home. He was returning from two years at Oxford University in England as a Rhodes scholar.

I'm sure that both King David and Pastor Rogness were overcome with many feelings, one of which must have surely been, "What might have been?"

Twenty years later, Pastor Rogness put some of his thoughts down about the event. They are timeless words about grief — authentic and universal. I'm sure we can extrapolate their spirit to the thoughts of King David when his son Absalom died. More important, perhaps they will speak for someone who grieves today at the loss of a loved one:

> *It isn't as if grief ever quite lets go. But now, except for some swift, unexpected moments, when the loss surges in upon me again, the wrenching pain is gone. Some of life's mirth and merriment may be gone too. But sorrow becomes more like a minor chord in a symphony which, with the jubilant majors, combines to make a rich melody.*
>
> *We do not belabor Paul's memory, nor avoid it. I occasionally wear his sweaters. We keep his pictures on display. Even his oar is resting against our bookcase, the oar he used in the Henley Regatta in the summer of 1960. It is at Christmas time that we miss him most. There are no presents for him or from him, nor his Christmas letter.* We speak of what he might now have been doing. *Sometimes I ponder what pain he may have been spared.* *

— Alvin W. Rogness

Bret Harte once shared some powerful words. They speak for

**The Book of Comfort,* Emphasis Augsburg, 1979, p. 103.

all the human family and so will stand as long as King David's words of lament:

> *Of all the words*
>   *of tongue and pen,*
> *The saddest are these:*
>   *It might have been.*

Conclusion

It is false to believe that the unendurable can't be endured. But when grief comes over us like a fog, we do not know that. Perhaps that's why the Psalms, music and poetry speak to us especially well at times of sorrow. I like to fantasize that King David would have loved to sing this hymn along with us today when we are at church, removing the sharp edges from our pain:

> *Guide me ever, great Redeemer,*
> *Pilgrim through this barren land.*
> *I am weak, but you are mighty;*
> *Hold me with your powerful hand.*
> *Bread of heaven, bread of heaven,*
> *Feed me now and ever-more,*
> *Feed me now and ever-more.*

>   — *Lutheran Book of Worship, 343, First Stanza*

Prayer

> *O God, let the salt of our tears preserve our humanness.*

Proper 16 (August 21-27)
Ordinary Time 21
2 Samuel 23:1-7

An Unusual Legacy

Introduction

There are all kinds of documents that tell about a person's life. Resumes, autobiographies and biographies, obituaries. Generally, they are quite flattering and they skim the cream from a person's experiences. Failures, broken promises, crushed dreams and major faults are not stirred to the surface for the public to see. Our real lives, on the other hand, are a blend of good and evil, strength and weakness, hope and despair.

But there is another important document that makes up a part of our lives. A will. That which we bequeath to our families and to our world. Sometimes there isn't much money involved, but we all leave a legacy (whether we know it or not) by the lives we live.

Our narrative today, 2 Samuel 23:1-7, is often called "the last words of David." Whether he or some later writer composed these words doesn't really matter. They sum up some of what he brought to the world and they point the way forward. They give a glimpse for the people of Israel of what leadership and the kingdom can achieve. This legacy suggests the perpetuity of the house (dynasty) of David. They are words of assurance that God will dwell with his people. These are truly "famous last words." In them there are at least three themes: (1) David's words were good words because the Spirit of the Lord spoke through him (2 Samuel 23:2); (2) a glimpse of perfect leadership (2 Samuel 23:3-4); and (3) an everlasting relationship/covenant (2 Samuel 23:5).

1. Good words

Language specialists claim that the five sweetest phrases in the English language are: "I love you." "Dinner is served." "All is forgiven." "Sleep 'til noon." "Keep the change." And there are those who choose to add: "You've lost weight!"

Words are good if they add dignity and confidence to people. King David's words did that. The ascription of nearly half the psalms to David is testimony to the regard in which this "sweet singer of Israel" was held. (2 Samuel 23:1) If this shepherd/warrior/king/poet/musician left us nothing other than the great expression of confidence in God's protection — where the Lord is compared to a shepherd — it would be legacy enough. How many people have been comforted and given new hope by these words:

The Lord is my shepherd, I
   shall not want;
he makes me lie down in green
   pastures.
He leads me beside still waters;
   he restores my soul.
He leads me in paths of
   righteousness
for his name's sake.

Even though I walk through the
   valley of the shadow of death,
I fear no evil;
for thou art with me;
   thy rod and thy staff,
   they comfort me.

Thou preparest a table before me
   in the presence of my enemies;
thou anointest my head with oil,
   my cup overflows.
Surely goodness and mercy shall
   follow me
   all the days of my life;
and I shall dwell in the house

*of the Lord
for ever.*

— Psalm 23 (A psalm of David)

David's "good words" did (and do) what Job's words did (and do) — at least according to Job's friend, Eliphaz:

Your words have kept people on their feet.
(Job 4:4 — my paraphrasing)

David left a legacy of good words that encouraged and brought hope and life to people. He also left a legacy of . . .

2. Leadership

In a poetic and beautiful way, the writer of "David's Legacy" gives us a glimpse of what perfect leadership might achieve.

*When one rules justly over men,
   ruling in the fear of God,
he dawns on them like the morning light,
   like the sun shining forth upon a
      cloudless morning,
   like rain that makes grass to sprout
      from the earth.* (2 Samuel 23:3b-4)

Such an image! All of us can visualize the two universal sights of sun and rain — not the blistering heat of noon in tropical countries, nor the torrential and violent rains which come sporadically, but rather the gentle, nourishing effects of warmth and water. Sun and rain together work the miracle of natural growth. They are gifts of God for all. This is the sort of leadership David's legacy is talking about. This is the sort of leadership the world always needs.

True leaders are true to themselves, basically honest and open. We ought not aspire to leadership, but if it comes, we need to accept it — "being ourselves" as we do lead. One of my favorite theologians, the cartoonist Charles Schulz, gives us a glimpse of this authenticity through one of his characters in Charlie Brown's gang.

In one "Peanuts" comic strip Lucy comes up to Charlie Brown and says, "Yes sir, Charlie Brown, would you like to have been Abraham Lincoln?"

"Well, now, I don't think so," he replies slowly; "I'm having a hard enough time being just plain Charlie Brown." I love it! I love it! God does not expect us to be persons other than ourselves. But he does expect us to make full use of our given abilities and to live lives of integrity and faithfulness wherever we are in our little corner of the earth.

Even though he slipped and fell short of perfect leadership, David gave us a glimpse of "what could be." And God was able to use his leadership to move his kingdom along. We can't be David, or Abraham Lincoln, or Dorothy Day or Shirley Chisholm. But we *can* be Roger. Or Shirley. For we, too, are a part of God's plan for his world.

3. Relationship/Covenant

Yea, does not my house stand so with God?
For he has made with me an everlasting covenant,
ordered in all things and secure. (2 Samuel 23:5)

With all the trouble we humans have with relationships (read that "covenants") these words fall on us like water in a desert. They are refreshing and life-giving.

God's everlasting covenant with us, culminating in the life, death and resurrection of Jesus the Christ, is a "base" for all our other covenants/relationships in this life.

As my mom approached her death, she continued to have a simple and clear trust in God. After she died we found the following piece in her Bible. It must have been her covenant with her Creator as she moved through the sunset of her life:

Lord, Thou knowest I am growing older. Keep me from the idea that I must express myself on every subject. Release me from the craving to meddle in everyone's affairs. Keep my tongue from the recital of endless details of the past which do not interest others. Seal my lips when I am inclined to talk about my aches and pains. They are increasing with the years, and my love to speak of them grows sweeter as time goes by. Teach me the glorious lesson that occasionally I may be wrong. Make me thoughtful, but not interfering; helpful, but not bossy. With the wisdom and experience I've gained, it does seem a pity not to use it all, but Thou knowest, Lord, that I want a few friends left at the end. So help me to pray more, talk less. And beyond all this, let me continue to flourish spiritually and bring fruit to Thy glory even in old age. AMEN

Not a bad "covenant" for us all as our day to "meet our Maker" approaches. And underneath this covenant, and David's covenant, and all the rest of them, are "the everlasting arms" of the living God. We give thanks daily for that.

Conclusion

King David left for posterity his good words, his leadership, and perhaps most of all, his "covenant" with God and the human family. Each of us can do the same — by God's grace — in our little corner of the world.

How shall we love you, holy, hidden Being,
   If we love not the world which you have made?
Oh, give us deeper love for better seeing
   Your Word made flesh, and in a manger laid.
Your kingdom come, O Lord; your will be done!*

Prayer

O God, in your mind the past and the future meet in this day. Help us to accept with grace what we have received, and to share all that — and more — with those to come.

**Lutheran Book of Worship,* No. 413, Stanza 5. This version in the LBW is altered from the original with permission of Oxford University Press, London, England.

Acknowledgments

Grateful acknowledgment is made to the following publishers and authors:

The Best of Stillmeadow, by Gladys Taber, J. B. Lippincott/Harper & Row, Copyright, 1976. Used by permission.

Blessed is the Ordinary, by Gerhard E. Frost. Copyright 1980 Gerhard E. Frost. Published by Winston Press, Inc., 430 Oak Grove, Minneapolis, Minnesota 55403. All rights reserved. Used with permission.

The Book of Comfort, by Alvin Rogness. Copyright, 1979, Augsburg Publishing House. Reprinted by permission.

The Deserted Rooster, by Ric Masten, Sunflower Ink, Palo Colorado Road. Carmel, California 93923. Copyright, 1982. Used by permission of the author.

"Ever to Be a Child," poem by Toyohiko Kagawa. Used by permission of Sumimoto Kagawa, The Kagawa Foundation, Tokyo, Japan.

Five Smooth Stones, by Eugene H. Peterson, John Knox Press, Copyright, 1980. Used by permission.

Freedom for Ministry, by Richard John Neuhaus, Harper & Row, Copyright 1979. Used by permission.

Johnny, We Hardly Knew Ye, by Kenneth O'Donnell and David F. Powers, Little, Brown & Company, Copyright, 1972. Used by permission.

Lutheran Book of Worship, Published by Augsburg Publishing House and Board of Publication, Lutheran Church in America, Copyright, 1978. Quoted texts used by permission.

Making Tracks, by Dennis Benson, Abingdon Press, Copyright, 1979. Used by permission of the author.

"Meditations for a Young Boy Confirmed," by Alan Paton. Copyright, 1954 Christian Century Foundation. Reprinted by permission, from the October 13, 1954 issue of The Christian Century magazine.

Men To Match My Mountains, by Irving Stone. Copyright 1956 by Irving Stone. Reprinted by permission of Doubleday & Company, Inc.

"Father Eternal, Ruler of Creation" Hymn number 413 in the *Lutheran Book of Worship.* Copyright by Oxford University Press, London, England. (The version in LBW is altered from the original text — Stanza 5 — By Laurence Housman (1865-1959).

Peculiar Treasure, by Frederick Buechner, Copyright 1979 by Frederick Buechner. Used by permission of Harper & Row, Publishers, Inc.

The Poetry of Robert Frost, edited by Edward Connery Lathem. Copyright, 1923, © 1969, by Holt, Rinehart and Winston. Copyright, 1951 by Robert Frost. Reprinted by permission of Holt, Rinehart and Winston, Publishers.

The Sacred Journey, by Frederick Buechner. Copyright 1982 by Frederick Buechner. Used by permission of Harper & Row, Publishers, Inc.

When Bad Things Happen to Good People, by Harold S. Kushner, Copyright, 1981, Schocken Books, Inc. Used by permission.

Wishful Thinking, by Frederick Buechner, Copyright 1979 by Frederick Buechner. Used by permission of Harper & Row, Publishers, Inc.